The Adventures of Odysseus

from *The Odyssey* by Homer
retold by Martin Waddell

ODYSSEUS AND THE LOTUS EATERS

After the fall of Troy, the Greeks sailed back to Greece in triumph, but when they got there, Odysseus wasn't with them.

He didn't turn up for another ten years.

"Where have you been?" his friends asked. "I tried to get home as fast as I could," said the cunning Odysseus, and he told them about his adventures.

THE ADVENTURES OF ODYSSEUS

When Troy fell, the Greeks destroyed the city, killing as many men as they could before they sailed home. Odysseus sailed with them, but his ships were scattered by storms. His men had a terrible time, until at last they came to the island of the Lotus Eaters.

It looked a lovely island. There were fig trees, and blue water rippled up on the beach, gleaming in the sun.

Odysseus allowed only three of his best men to land.

The Lotus Eaters were happy, smiling, sleepy-eyed people. They set the three men down beneath a fig tree, and brought them wine and food.

The sailors tasted the food. It was lovely. "What's this made from?" they asked.

"The Lotus plant," replied the Lotus Eaters. "Do have some more."

"Don't mind if we do," said the sailors.

The sailors who had stayed on the ship began to grumble. "They're lazing about having a good time, and we're stuck out here fixing the ships!"

"Do you want to see your wives and your children again?" Odysseus asked them.

"Of course we do," said the sailors.

"So do our friends on the beach," said cunning Odysseus. "But something in that food has weakened their brains. If they don't leave with us, they will never see home again. We have to save them for the sake of *their* wives and *their* children."

That was the end of their Lotus eating. Odysseus set sail for home.

Odysseus and the Cyclops

Odysseus and the Greek sailors came to an island inhabited by Cyclopes. The Cyclopes weren't a bit like the Lotus Eaters. They were huge giants with one eye each, in the centre of their foreheads. They spent their time looking after very big sheep … when they weren't killing people, and eating them that is.

"I'll go in with one ship *only*," Odysseus decided, "and we won't attack them unless we have to. We'll bring them a cask of wine as a gift, and try being friendly instead."

The sailors landed on the island, but didn't see anyone. They came to a place where the hillsides were honeycombed with large caves, and they went into one. Then …

The Cyclops sealed the door of the cave with a stone. They were trapped!

"Kill him when he's sleeping!" the sailors told Odysseus.

"*Great idea*," said Odysseus. "If I kill him who is going to roll back the big stone at the mouth of the cave? We'd be caught in here with his body, and some other Cyclops would turn up and make minced-Greek of us."

Next morning, the Cyclops ate two more sailors for breakfast, picked the scraps of sailor out of his teeth with a well-nibbled thigh bone, and set off with his enormous sheep, leaving the captured Greeks in the cave … and Odysseus got busy.

He took a tree trunk that the Cyclops used as a staff.

"Sharpen one end," he told his men. "Then season it in the fire, so it won't break when I use it."

"What for?" asked the sailors.

"Wait and see," said Odysseus.

THE ADVENTURES OF ODYSSEUS

The Cyclops came back that evening, and ate two more sailors for supper.

Odysseus came towards him, holding out the cask of wine. "You'll like this," he told the Cyclops. "It will go down well after all the sailors you've been eating."

The Cyclops drank the wine. It was *good* wine.

"What's your name?" he asked, wiping his lips.

"Nobody," said Odysseus, carefully.

"Well, *Nobody* … as a reward for this wine, I'll save eating you until after I've eaten all the others," the Cyclops said with a horrible grin. "Isn't that nice of me?"

Then he went to sleep.

Odysseus and four of his men pushed the tree trunk into the fire and kept it there until it was red hot. Then they thrust it into the Cyclops' one eye.

The blinded Cyclops howled and sobbed with pain and anger. His horrible screams alerted the others, who were sleeping in their caves nearby.

"Who blinded you?" they called to him.

"Nobody! Nobody!" he shouted to them.

"That's all right then," the monsters outside decided. "If nobody did it, it must be the will of the gods."

They yawned and stretched and turned round and went back to bed.

The Cyclops was left inside his cave, playing Blindman's Buff with the sailors … being torn to pieces and eaten was the prize for anyone who got caught, and the sailors didn't enjoy it. They hid among the giant sheep, so the Cyclops couldn't find them.

In the end the game stopped.

THE ADVENTURES OF ODYSSEUS

The Cyclops rolled the big stone from the mouth of the cave, and called his flock of sheep out.

He felt the back of each sheep as it passed to make sure that the frightened sailors didn't creep out with the sheep.

"Now he's taken the sheep away, we won't be able to hide amongst them. When that horrible Cyclops comes back he will eat us."

"Don't worry" said Odysseus. "I've got a plan."

He divided the huge sheep into groups of three, and he made each man hide *under* a number two sheep, the one in the middle.

The Cyclops stroked the back and the sides of each sheep as it passed, but he didn't stroke underneath and so the sailors escaped out of the cave. "We're out!" cried the sailors.

They fled back to their ship, and sailed off to join the rest of Odysseus' fleet.

"No more risks! We want to go home right now," the scared sailors said to Odysseus.

"Me too," sighed Odysseus.

ODYSSEUS AND THE BAG OF FOUL WINDS

The next place the Greek sailors landed was friendly. The king who lived there had been blessed by the gods. He promised Odysseus fair winds that would carry him and his sailors home and gave him a stout leather bag, tied tightly with a string made of silver.

"Don't let this leave your sight for a minute," he told Odysseus. "All the foul winds that blow are held in it. If the winds are let out of the bag, you'll be wrecked and you will never get home."

Odysseus went back on board with the bag but he wouldn't let anyone touch it.

"It is treasure he's found on our travels," the sailors decided. "We want our share."

For nine days Odysseus didn't sleep, and the fair winds kept up, taking them home ... but at last he was so tired that he slept.

"Now's our chance," said the men, and they crept up to the sleeping Odysseus, and loosened the string round the neck of the bag.

The winds *whooshed* out of the bag blowing the ships off course.

"Where's this wind blowing us to?" wailed the sailors.

"I'll tell you where it's not blowing us to!" said the angry Odysseus. "It's not blowing us home."

The foul winds blew them to an island. It had a safe harbour with great cliffs around it that would shield the ships from the sea.

"The foul winds blew us here. I'm not going to land," Odysseus said, and he kept his own ship far off shore.

The rest of the ships entered the harbour and anchored. The islanders began throwing huge boulders from the cliff tops. The ships were wrecked, and the islanders killed the sailors as they swam towards the shore.

"At least we escaped with our lives, by staying out here," Odysseus told his own crew.

"You've lost all the ships but this one!" moaned the sailors.

"Don't blame me," muttered Odysseus. "I didn't open the bag of foul winds!"

ODYSSEUS AND THE PIG SAILORS

"You take a look first," the Greek sailors said to Odysseus, the next time they came to land on an island.

Odysseus climbed a high hill. From the top of the hill he could see a great forest, and the towers of a palace.

"Half of you go through the forest and explore," Odysseus ordered. "The other half stay with me here, near the ship."

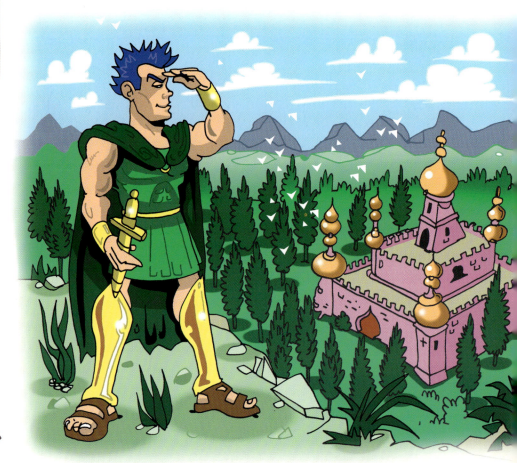

THE ADVENTURES OF ODYSSEUS

They went on through the forest, towards the great palace, but then they found themselves surrounded by fierce beasts. There were lions and tigers and wolves all around them.

The men started shouting and throwing spears at the wolves.

The wolves chased the spears and brought them back to the sailors, like pet dogs playing fetch-the-stick.

Then a lion came up, and licked someone's hand.

One of the tigers wanted a sailor to tickle his tummy.

"They're all tame!" gasped the sailors, and they travelled on.

As they drew near to the palace they heard soft music playing, and young maidens singing sweet songs of love.

"Oh boy!" thought the sailors.

A beautiful princess called Circe came to welcome them. She led them into her palace and sat them down to a feast of fine wine and gorgeous food.

"This is the life!" the sailors thought but …

Each sailor Circe trapped turned into a pig.

THE ADVENTURES OF ODYSSEUS

"I promised we'd rescue them if things went wrong," said Odysseus, when he heard what had happened. He set off to rescue his men.

A strange boy met him in the forest. He seemed to know who Odysseus was, although they'd never met. He said he'd been sent by the goddess Athena, who took special care of Odysseus.

"This will guard you from Circe's magic!" he said, and he gave Odysseus a sprig of a plant called Moly, which is like the wild garlic that people once used to fight vampires with.

Odysseus came to Circe's palace and she welcomed him in and gave him good food and wine, just as she'd done with his men.

Then she tapped him with her wand.

"Pig ... go in the sty like the rest!" she said ... But the sprig of Moly stopped her magic from working.

Odysseus raised his sword to cut off her head, but she fell on her knees and pleaded for mercy.

"Turn my sailors back into men ... or else!" said Odysseus.

Circe vowed that she would, and she did ... not only that, she helped the Greeks with the work they had to do on their ships.

THE ADVENTURES OF ODYSSEUS

ODYSSEUS AND THE FOUR DANGERS

The Greeks sailed away from Circe's island.

"Why is Odysseus so worried?" the sailors asked. "We're going home!"

"Circe didn't want him to go, so she has told him stories of all kinds of monsters we're likely to meet on the way," one of them said. "That's my guess anyway."

Then Odysseus started giving them orders.

"Put wax in our ears?" gasped the sailors. "What for?"

"Never you mind," said Odysseus. "And the other bit is … you have to tie me to the mast, and not let me loose till we're past the next island, whatever happens."

THE ADVENTURES OF ODYSSEUS

Circe had warned Odysseus of the Sirens, sea nymphs whose strange, beautiful singing bewitched sailors so much that they leapt into the sea and drowned themselves.

As the Greeks sailed past the island, the sound of sweet singing came from over the sea … but only Odysseus could hear it. He was bewitched by the sound, and tried to dive into the waves. The ropes held him fast, and the ship sailed on, until the danger had passed.

"One danger past, three dangers to go!" Odysseus told the sailors. "We have to sail through a narrow channel where there is a great whirlpool, called Charybdis. It sucks the sea in three times a day. If we're caught in that whirlpool … we drown."

"If we see the water suddenly stir, we'll get out of the way," the men decided.

"That's not all," said Odysseus. "A monster called Scylla lives in the rocks close by the channel. She has six heads, and six long necks. She scoops sailors out of their ships, and eats them."

They had to sail on, but they sailed slowly and carefully.

From far away they could hear the great whirlpool roar, and as they drew nearer it grew worse.

"Concentrate on the sea!" warned Odysseus. "If you see it start to surge …"

But it was the monster Scylla that got them.

The sailors wailed and cried for help as they were eaten. There was nothing Odysseus could do.

"Watching the sea, we forgot all about Scylla the monster!" Odysseus groaned, blaming himself.

They still had to meet the last danger.

"Next we come to the Isle of the Sun," Odysseus told his men. "We'll only stay for the time that it takes to load water and food on the ship. Circe warned me that we would be destroyed if we harm the cows."

They landed, but the tides and winds turned against them and they were forced to stay. Soon they had eaten all the fruit and vegetables that grew on the island.

"Eat the fish and the birds!" ordered Odysseus. "Don't go near the cows."

"I'm fed up eating bird pie and stewed fish. I really fancy a nice juicy steak," a sailor said one day when Odysseus was out of the way.

They looked at the cows.

"Steak on legs!" they said to each other.

When Odysseus returned, he found his sailors sprawled on the shore, with a cow roasting on their fire. They were stuffing themselves full of steaks that they had cut from the cow.

Odysseus was terrified, because everything else that Circe had told him had come true. It seemed to him that the cow's skin crawled on the ground and the dead cow on the spit mooed as it roasted.

THE ADVENTURES OF ODYSSEUS

"As soon as we put to sea we'll be killed!" moaned Odysseus.

And that's just what happened. There was a great storm and the ship sank. All the steak-eating sailors were drowned … but Odysseus escaped.

Odysseus clung to a raft while the storm lasted, and the waves blew him to the shore of a beautiful island.

He stayed there for a very long time, with a lovely sea nymph called Calypso, who looked after him until he got his strength back. Then he sailed on and had more adventures, until he landed alone on the shore near his home.

"Home at last!" sighed Odysseus … but there was one more danger to face.

Odysseus and the Arrows

"Odysseus will come back to us soon," Penelope, Odysseus' wife had told his son, Telemachus. But Odysseus didn't come. Long years went by, and the boy grew into a man, without ever seeing his father.

"Odysseus must be dead. Whoever marries his beautiful wife will do well," decided the princes from Odysseus' kingdom. They came to the island where Odysseus had lived, hoping to marry her. With only her young son to protect her, Penelope was helpless. The princes all settled down to wait in the best rooms in the palace.

THE ADVENTURES OF ODYSSEUS

"You must find your father," Penelope warned her son, "or the princes will force me to marry one of them."

Telemachus went to many places but he couldn't find Odysseus. He came back to his home island, and an old man in rags was waiting for him. "Be careful, my son," warned the old man. "Your mother's suitors are planning to kill you, when you return to the palace."

"Don't 'my son' me!" Telemachus said. "You're not my father!"

"Oh yes I am," said the ragged old beggar, and Odysseus whipped off his disguise. "These men plan to force your mother to take one of them as her husband," he told his son. "I've been with them, but in disguise. Only my old dog recognised me. He was very old, but bounded up to me wagging his tail like a puppy. Then he died at my feet. Your mother's guests treated me like a dirty old tramp while they were feasting and drinking at my own table. But we'll settle that score!"

The first thing Odysseus and Telemachus did was to collect the weapons from everybody in the palace and store them in the armoury.

"Why should we give you our weapons?" the princes' ringleader asked Telemachus.

"My mother will marry. I am taking your weapons to stop you fighting each other over the result. There's to be an archery trial in the Great Hall," Telemachus told the ringleader. "You'll be asked to fire an arrow from my father's old bow through twelve rings made from axes, set in a straight row. Whoever succeeds in that task, my mother will marry."

THE ADVENTURES OF ODYSSEUS

The next day the princes gathered in the Great Hall. Odysseus' servants barred the doors from the outside, and the contest began. No one had enough strength to even bend Odysseus' great bow …

"Let me try," said the old ragged beggar, and everyone laughed. Odysseus bent the bow effortlessly, and the arrow sped straight through the rings.

"Now for another mark!" said Odysseus, and an arrow sped to the heart of the ringleader, who fell dead on the floor.

"Who wants to die first?" Odysseus asked, taking aim.

The hero had come home at last!